Make Money Online Entrepreneur Series:
Book 10
List Building with LinkedIn

KIP PIPER

http://www.kippiperbooks.com

YOUR FREE GIFT…

Want a free book? Want access to more freebies and special offers through Amazon?

As a way of saying *thanks* for your purchase, I'm offering a free eBook that is only available to my customers. Right now, you can get a copy of my book: *"28-Day Small Business Profit Plan: The Quick Start Guide for Business Success"*. This book is not sold anywhere else and can only be found on my website.

Plus, you will learn how to get instant notification whenever there is a **new free book** or **special book bundles** through Amazon.

Get the details at my website: **www.KipPiperBooks.com**

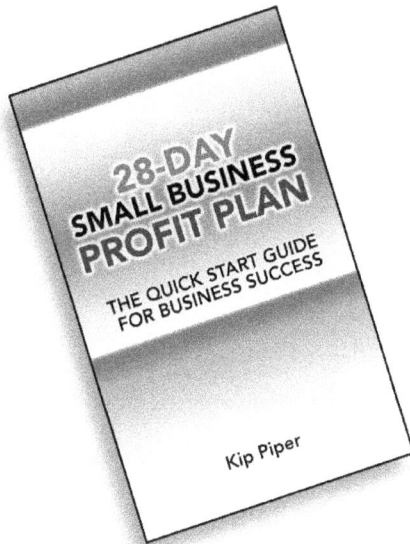

CONTENTS

AUTHOR'S NOTE

As you have probably experienced, the Internet and the websites on it are constantly changing. The information, examples, and screenshots presented in this book are accurate at the time of publication.

If you encounter any websites that have changed, please let me know by emailing me at: kip@kippiperbooks.com.

Remember, even though the website(s) may have changed, the principles, techniques and strategies in this book remain sound.

For your convenience, all websites, tools, and software mentioned in this book are listed in the RESOURCES section at the end of this book.

The links provided are primarily affiliate links, which means if you purchase through the links, the price is the same to you and I receive a commission. This is the heart of affiliate marketing and entrepreneurship – which I am teaching you how to do with this book! I thank you in advance for using the affiliate links.

A FEW WORDS FROM KIP

Before I began teaching others how to blog and be successful with their online businesses, I wanted to be sure that I had something different to teach – strategies that are not easily found but can make a huge impact on success. The last thing I wanted to do is waste anyone's time. I wanted to offer something unique that would add both value and the potential for quick success for you.

Unknowingly, my research into online business success began in 1996 when I was first introduced to the concept of affiliate marketing. The potential for income excited me and I was quick to start experimenting with it. I joined Amazon.com and the few other affiliate programs available at the time. I added links on my website to products that related to my web design and Internet marketing business, with the purpose of offering quality resources to my website visitors and my clients. I encouraged and worked with my clients to include affiliate marketing in their overall online presence. I did this all in the hopes of adding to my income streams and eventually have affiliate marketing my dominant, if not sole, source of income.

But it did not come quickly, as others had promised or experienced. I totally, 100% believed in the concept of an online business and affiliate marketing (and still do), I understood the mechanics of setting up websites, creating products, and adding affiliate links, but I struggled with ranking my site high with the search engines and driving traffic to my site. Where were all the promised visitors who would buy what I offered or recommended so I could earn commissions?

Why were so many others achieving success? Why wasn't I experiencing the same success? Where was I going wrong?

I joined various mastermind groups. I purchased training programs from so-called "gurus". I bought books, read articles, watched videos, attended conference calls and webinars – I immersed myself in learning about blogging, affiliate marketing, and creating products.

The one most important thing I learned is that you need multiple websites, each focused on a different niche, to ensure a steady stream of income. "But," I asked, "if I can't get people to come to my first website, why should I spend more money and time creating websites that will not be visited either?" And each "guru" smiled nicely and said, "If you will upgrade your membership to our most expensive level, I'll tell you." But when I looked closely, I realized each "guru" was not living the life I wanted. In fact, most were working as hard or harder than I – with even less free time and income! They did not have the freedom of time and money that I wanted.

I didn't give up, though. I continued my search – knowing the one little "missing link" was out there.

One day I found it!

With this new knowledge, I knew without a doubt I could not only be personally successful with blogging, affiliate marketing and product creation, but now I could teach others those same strategies.

I realized that knowledge is what sets apart the training I offer – with this book and my other books which you can find at **http://www.kippiperbooks.com**.

This book is unique because it was written for *YOU*.

- YOU are someone who sees the potential in having an online business of affiliate marketing and product creation, but needs to know how to get started.
- YOU want practical strategies and advice that have already been tested and proven to work.
- YOU are ready for double-digit growth in sales.
- YOU are committed to following through with what you're about to learn.

This is why YOU are here.

Now please understand. Every piece of advice, strategy and practice has been tested on actual live blog, affiliate marketing and product websites – my own, my clients', and others. None of this is theory. You might then ask yourself, *ok, so how many blogs and affiliate websites has Kip done and what qualifies her as an "internet business expert"?* I think that's a great question. I wish more people questioned so called "experts" to see what qualifies them. As for me, I looked back on the last 15 years of stats and discovered that I have personally generated a 5-figure income in blogging, affiliate marketing and my own product sales – and that's just part-time!

If that's something you'd like to accomplish, you've selected the right book and series to begin with. I say "begin" because you'll soon discover that the learning process is a journey.

But don't worry! There's one more thing that qualifies me to lead you down this path – I'm just like you. It doesn't matter if you've never built a website or if you're already earning an income with blogging, affiliate marketing and your own product, and simply want to improve your sales. As you have already read, I've been wherever you are right now.

For anyone who reads this book and the entire *"Make Money Online Entrepreneur Series"*, and implements everything they learn, I can guarantee your business will move forward with more subscribers, sales and a stronger connection to your market. Like I said before, it doesn't matter if you've never built a website in your life or if you're already experienced, I've been there and can show you how to make blogging, affiliate marketing and product creation a successful income source.

But before we begin, I need you to do something. Connect with me on Facebook at:

http://www.facebook.com/TheRandomBlondeFanPage

I'd love to stay in touch and learn more about your journey.

You also are invited to check my website for more business books, and all of the books included in this *"Making Money Online Entrepreneur Series"*:

http://www.kippiperbooks.com

Thanks again for choosing to spend this time with me. Now let's get started!

"Done is better than Perfect!"

INTRODUCTION

This is Book 10 of the "Make Money Online Entrepreneur Series": "List Building with LinkedIn".

The entire series consists of more than 20 books, specifically written as an entire online business success training course.

Beginning in August 2013, I released one book about every two weeks, in the proper order to ensure success. If you follow the series from Book 1 to the end, one week per book, you will complete a 12-month training course and master being an online entrepreneur! Of course, you can finish the series faster. Just make sure you fully complete the lessons in each book before moving on to the next. This way your success will be greater!

This series is carefully designed to give you every building block you need to build a successful online business. All of the guesswork is taken away, and by following this series, you will avoid most of the common mistakes made by new and even experienced online entrepreneurs. All is revealed – nothing is left out!

The beauty of this series is that you can pick up any book on whatever topic you need at this moment. Or you can purchase each book as it is released. Or ultimately, you can purchase the entire series in a bundle!

However you choose to use the information offered in this and the other books, you will be moving forward with intention and strategy for success in your business.

If at any time you have questions or desire personal one-on-one coaching for a particular topic, feel free to contact me at kip@kippiperbooks.com.

Here's to your online business success!

ONLINE BUSINESS SUCCESS CORE VALUES

Before we get started, it is important to understand, to be a successful online business entrepreneur, it is necessary that you stay focused on your business and have the core values that ensure that success. Here are the values that I have found to be essential to keeping focused and moving forward. These values will be at the beginning of every book of this *"Make Money Online Entrepreneur Series"*.

Be Passionate About Entrepreneurship

As it says, you need to be passionate about what you do and about being an entrepreneur. Being an entrepreneur will present the greatest challenges and the greatest joy you've ever experienced in the business world.

Commit 100% And GO FOR IT

One of the biggest things about being successful is being okay with putting yourself out there. Even if it's just a part-time business, commit 100% of yourself to the time you invest in your business. Commit to see it through and don't give up too soon. As the saying goes, "Don't give up before the miracle happens." Be patient and be persistent.

Build A Network of Support & influence

You must build a network of support and influence. This means building your Facebook community, building your Twitter community, and building your LinkedIn community. You must contribute to other people and help them be successful. By contributing to others and helping them be successful, you will become successful.

Get Comfortable with Being Uncomfortable

You're going to be doing a lot of things that you may or may not have done in the past. You can only grow when you're uncomfortable. When you're feeling comfortable and used to doing the things that you normally do, it's really difficult to grow, so you need to be comfortable with being uncomfortable see you can stretch and grow.

Consistent Growth & Improvement

It is important that you commit to consistent growth and improvement. We all need improvement especially if we are to grow and become successful, because staying up to date with the current tools and resources is essential. What helps you with consistent growth and continuing to improve is tracking your progress on irregular basis.

You also need to be okay with evaluating yourself and looking back at what you did and what you didn't do – without judgment. Simply observe and then recommit to the next step of growth and improvement.

80/20 Rule & Speed of Implementation

I'm sure you would've heard of the 80/20 rule (also known as Pareto's Rule) that 20% of what you do provides 80% of your success. So you need to understand that not everything you do is going to be perfect. Learn from it and move on. The quicker you get things done with the knowledge that you have, the more you'll be able to grow.

Flexible Persistence

Be persistent with everything that you do, and stay consistent with everything you do. The ones who experience the most success are the ones who are persistent in accomplishing their goals and are the most consistent in what they do. To be consistent, you must commit to regularly completing the tasks that ensure your success, whether those tasks occur daily, weekly, monthly, etc.

Surround Yourself With "A" Players

In business you deserve to surround yourself with the best and those who share your entrepreneurial spirit. You become like those you spend your time with. So choose carefully who you hang around with, so you are with those who think like you and make you stretch and reach higher.

The same goes for your employees. If you're going to outsource, you must select the best people who are competent and people you will enjoy working with. Avoid people who have negative attitudes. Surround yourself with those who embrace the concepts of small business success, entrepreneurship, and financial wealth.

Sell With Conviction

Be passionate about your product or service. Make sure you understand every aspect of it so that you can easily describe its features and benefits to your potential customers. If you have hesitations or doubts about your product, improve it so you don't have doubts.

Celebrate All Wins

Celebrate all victories! When you get that first sale, celebrate that first sale. Celebrate each new client. Celebrate each year of business success. Make sure you celebrate all wins. This is really important to maintain passion, momentum and to ensure success.

INTRODUCTION TO LINKEDIN

In this book we're going to talk about all things LinkedIn.

LinkedIn is not like any other social media network out there. The reason for this is because LinkedIn is widely regarded the most professional social network out there. So no matter what is your business, the people that are on LinkedIn have a profile because they are looking to network in a professional sense.

So let's think about how this relates to our business.

If we're an Internet or information marketer and we're trying to attract consumer customers, LinkedIn is not the best venue. Instead, Facebook and Twitter are best for tracking consumer customers. (See my books *List Building with Facebook* and *List Building with Twitter* to learn how successfully use these venues to attract consumer customers.)

If we are a business-to-business relationship provider or Internet marketer – meaning we're selling to businesses rather than individual consumers – then we probably are going to have a huge benefit by being part of LinkedIn because we can connect directly with our potential business customers.

So make sure you understand but LinkedIn is and what LinkedIn isn't – as how to best leverage it and how your product of service fits in there.

To recap, if you're selling to businesses – and it doesn't matter if it's a multinational company with 10,000 employees or a single entrepreneur company or anything in between – if you're selling to someone who identifies themselves as a business owner or the manager of a business or the decision maker for a business, then you're going to be able to sell directly to these potential customers on LinkedIn.

If you're a business-to-consumer information or Internet marketer – for instance, you sell tips on how to train your dog – you're not going to necessarily find your potential customers on LinkedIn. You could possibly find the occasional dog kennel owner, but when all is considered, as a business-to-consumer marketer on LinkedIn you're more likely to find affiliate marketing and other types of relationships that you might leverage.

Make sure you understand what LinkedIn is and how to best you can best leverage it for your niche.

If you're not excited about LinkedIn, you need to be! By properly leveraging LinkedIn, it can provide you the avenues to generate a consistent and significant stream of income. As you go through this book, if you don't already understand about LinkedIn, you can have an individual profile, your company can have a page, but there are also LinkedIn groups. Groups are a big part of LinkedIn. You can create your own LinkedIn group, and with proper nurturing, you can grow this group become a major source of income for you and your business. When you own a LinkedIn group, you have the ability to send a direct text emails to that group – one a week. Over the course of a month, you can send four direct text emails that promote targeted offers.

Whether you're looking to build a group to which to sell directly, build a group with which to network, trying to find affiliates, or even trying to find potential customers you can sell two in the future, LinkedIn is a great way to be able to find and identify those people.

One of the things that is really important to understand about LinkedIn, as with other social networks, while you are able to promote affiliate offers and even your own offers within LinkedIn on your personal page, on your company page and within groups, you still want to be able to capture those connections and convert them to your email list – because that's your best point of monetization. If you can get people from your LinkedIn groups or from your profile or LinkedIn connections to your email list, it's very powerful because then you will be able to market directly to them in a targeted fashion.

As you go through this book, remember the focus is to get these connections to your email list. Also consider how your business fits into LinkedIn says people are identifying themselves as business professionals, which is different than other social media networks in that respect.

DEVELOP YOUR LINKEDIN STRATEGY

In these first three chapters, we're going to discuss what a lot of people tend to overlook but is important to consider and think about before you to dive into LinkedIn. This is all about starting your profile and going over the basics.

While the basics might seem like something you want to skip over, this section will help you understand what it is *you* want to get out of LinkedIn – figuring out your goals, with whom do you want to connect, and things like this. Determining these now will ensure faster success, more targeted results, and will help prevent wasting time.

These first three chapters – Develop Your Strategy, Creating a Profile From Scratch, and Navigating LinkedIn – cover the essential basics which are critical to your success.

So let's get started on developing your strategy before you even use LinkedIn.

Linked in is, in my opinion, the most powerful business social networking site on the Internet. There are millions of professionals on LinkedIn. At the time of this writing, there are over 259 million business professionals on LinkedIn. The average household income is over $110,000 per year and has twice the buying power of the average consumer. This is higher than any other social networking site's average user base.

So take all this in consideration when you realize that LinkedIn is a very powerful site *if you know how to use it right*.

What a lot of people do when they get on LinkedIn is say, "I'm going to create a profile and hope that people find me and I start getting business." After a few months and it doesn't happen for them, they got upset and say, "LinkedIn doesn't work for me! I'm supposed to be getting all these leads and sales and opportunities for my career, but it's not happening."

When you start with LinkedIn, you really need to have a strategy and initially dive into massive action. You must be active early on to get things going. Consider these things:

- What do you want to get out of your professional career or your business?
- Are you looking for a job?
- Are you trying to get more business leads?
- Are you trying to make more sales?
- Are you trying to get publicity?
- Are you trying to drive more ticket sales to your live events?
- What is it that you want to do?

You want to write these down and figure these out first before you actually start with LinkedIn. Once you know what you want to achieve in your business or professional career, then you can tailor your LinkedIn profile and your LinkedIn strategy around those goals you have.

Now if you already started with LinkedIn, don't despair! You will also learn in this book how to take your current LinkedIn profile and make it work for you. So still sit down right now, consider what you want to get out of LinkedIn and write down your goals.

When you write down your goals, it made a list of just one thing, such as, "I want to get a job." Or it can be "I want to make $1 million in sales in the next year." Once you have that clear goal of what you want to achieve, you can start utilizing the various resources and tools throughout LinkedIn. There are a lot of different things you can do on LinkedIn to achieve your goals. I'm going to show you what is available to help you achieve those goals.

So first is understanding what you want to get out of LinkedIn. Think of LinkedIn as a huge social networking site filled with millions of business professionals who are looking to do business as well. You and they have the same common mindset – when they come onto LinkedIn, they want to do business, they're looking for more business opportunities, they are looking to build their business and help others build theirs as well. It's different from the other social networking sites in that most people on here are in business and want to build their business.

Take a few minutes right now and write down your goals on how you want to utilize LinkedIn.

NAVIGATING LINKEDIN

In this chapter we're going to review navigating the LinkedIn website.

The homepage of LinkedIn is what you want to focus on the most. When you come to the homepage, you will see that LinkedIn focuses on the status update and network activity. It has a similar look and feel as Facebook and Twitter. You will see your newsfeed where people are posting their own status updates, links to different articles, and a variety of other things – similar to the Facebook wall. You are on Facebook, then you understand how this looks.

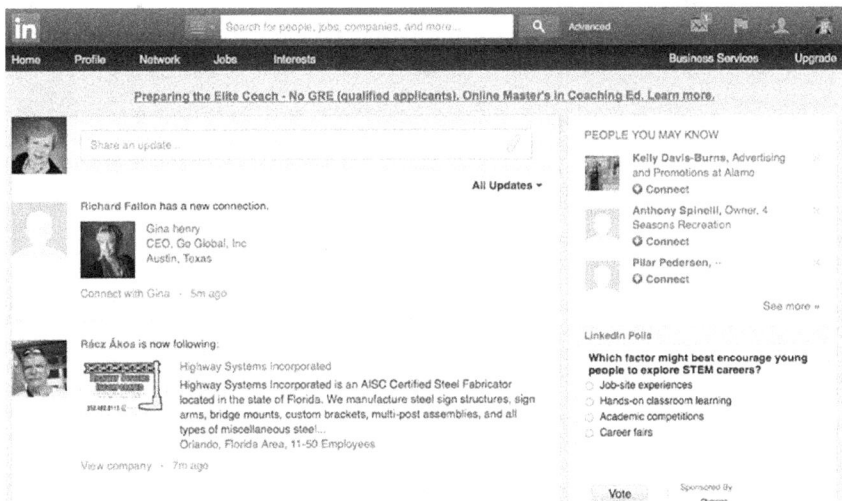

You can also sync your Twitter account to your LinkedIn account, so every time you post a tweet, it also gets posted on your LinkedIn account.

LinkedIn did not always have the status update and the newsfeed at the top of the homepage. The top of the homepage used to show who you were connected to, how to connect to new people and what people were doing in various groups. LinkedIn transitioned the homepage to have the status update and newsfeed at the top of the homepage. They are doing this for a reason – they are trying to keep up with the other popular social media sites, especially Facebook and Twitter. I think this is a smart thing! LinkedIn is growing and will continue to grow as the most powerful business social networking site on the Internet.

In this book, I'm going to show you how to maximize your homepage see you get lots of traffic to your site using one simple section – the status update – to share a link in your newsfeed and then to different LinkedIn groups. You could potentially share to hundreds of thousands of professionals tailored to your niche.

For right now, I'm going to quickly show you the basics of getting around LinkedIn.

First of all, the top menu is where you can access everything you need to navigate the LinkedIn website.

As you can see below, you hover the mouse over the top menu to access the different areas of each menu link. For example, you can hover the mouse over the "Profile" link in the top menu and then click on "Edit Profile" to see and edit your profile. (Your profile is a very powerful factor in how successfully you're able to leverage LinkedIn.)

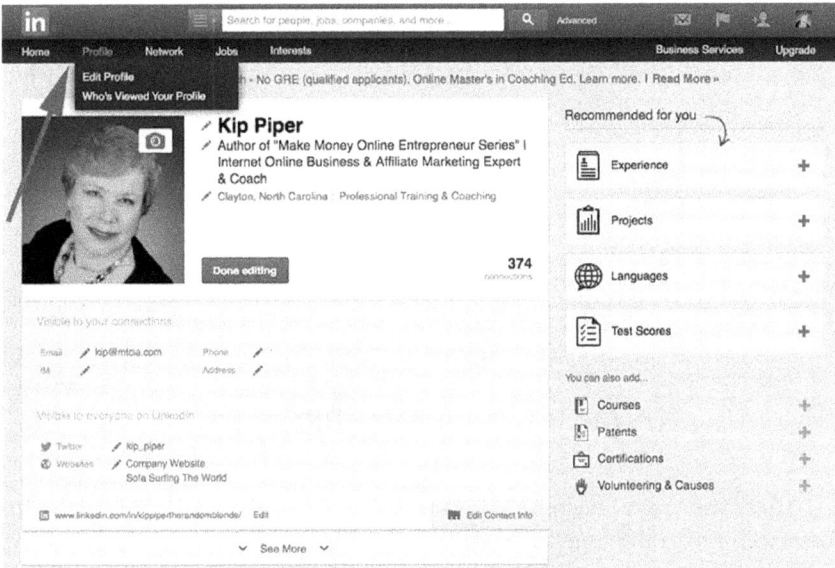

Navigating the top menu is pretty basic, however there is so much more information available than what you typically find in either Facebook or Twitter. There is a lot of different functionality with LinkedIn.

Since the LinkedIn interface is regularly changing, I'm not going to go over each menu item at this time. I encourage you to wander around the website for a few minutes, clicking on different menu items, and becoming familiar with their location and how to access them. In the coming lessons I will be talking about the specific areas of LinkedIn, so you will need to be able to find each section.

YOUR LINKEDIN PROFILE

After you have become familiar with the once you join LinkedIn interface, now is the time to create your profile.

Whether you're new to LinkedIn or you have completed some of your profile on LinkedIn. you need to make sure you have completed your profile 100%.

LinkedIn will ask you for a lot of basic information. Of course there is the obvious, such as, your first and last name, a headline for your profile, your current and past work experience, your education, etc.

Next, LinkedIn will ask you to add some connections. They will also ask you to ask your website(s).

LinkedIn will ask you to write a summary, your specialties, etc.

As you complete the different steps, LinkedIn will tell you how far along you are in the process of completing your profile. LinkedIn will also offer suggestions on what you can do to either finish your profile or improve your profile. If you already have a LinkedIn profile, the process status will tell you what you may still be missing.

While this seems like a daunting assignment, especially if you've been in the professional world for any length of time, it is well worth your time and effort to complete this now. Yes, you can always go back and edit or update your information, but before going any further, take the time to complete this now. It will make a significant difference in how effective and successful you are in the future steps. Completing your profile now will make sure that you establish the proper connections and influence in the LinkedIn groups that you join and create – and directly impact on your online business success.

So stop right now – do not proceed to the next chapter – until you've taken the time to complete your profile 100%. *Please trust me that this is any social step for your online business success.*

CREATE A COMPELLING HEADLINE

Now that you completed your profile, we will begin the advanced profile optimization.

If you have not completed your profile 100%, go do that now! Failing to do so before proceeding to this chapter and future chapters will mean that you are wasting your time and potentially negatively impacting your online business success.

In this chapter we will create your compelling headline. A compelling headline is critical because it is the first thing that people see when they come to your profile.

When you first go to your "Edit Profile" section, as seen below, you must make sure you have your first and last name *only*. LinkedIn has changed its terms of service and no longer allows keywords, descriptive phrases, and similar items in your name field. You take the risk of getting banned by LinkedIn if you list anything more than just your first and last name.

The professional headline, as seen below, is one of the most important elements of your LinkedIn profile. We make a lot of opinions the first time we see something or the first time we meet someone. We make opinions from their appearance, what they say, their body language, etc. This is also true when it comes to your LinkedIn profile. The first time and lands on your LinkedIn profile page, you want them to have a good first impression on you as an individual, as a professional, as a businessperson, etc.

The perceived value – good impression – is more important than the actual real value that you have to give. You want to make your profile and first impression as clean as possible. Obviously, you don't want to lie and make up things that are not true, but you to put your best foot forward. It's similar to a resume where you put the best of your experience and education in the most influential language and still true about yourself.

As you can see (at the time of this writing), my professional headline is "Author of 'Make Money Online Entrepreneur Series' | Internet Online Business & Affiliate Marketing Expert & Coach". There is more I could add, but LinkedIn limits the number of characters in the headline. They offer some examples of what you could put. But for a compelling headline, those examples or not good enough.

When creating your compelling headline, you want to think about a few different things. Take into account that you want to tell people who you are, who you help, and how you help them. (By the way, this is something you should do throughout your whole profile – tell people who you are, who you help, and how to help them.)

I put a lot of emphasis on the headline because this is the first thing people see when they are searching for a business coach or a marketing consultant or IT professional, etc. These are the terms that people will type into the search bar, and if your profile appears in the first five results – or even number one (and I'll show you how to do that) – want to be sure that your headline gives them the proper idea on what you do and how you can help them right then. If you don't tell them how you can help them right then, they will scroll down the list and find somebody else. You want simply click on *your* profile.

If possible, include a call to action in your headline so people want to click on your profile and read more. The more attention you can keep on your profile the better, and the better chance you will get business out of it.

Since I have a number of different projects, all related to online business and affiliate marketing, I first show that I am the author of this *Make Money Online Entrepreneurs Series*, then identify myself as an expert and coach. It breaks down this way:

- Who I am: an author, expert, coach
- Who do I help: anyone in Internet online business and affiliate marketing
- How do I help them: through my books and as a coach

I could also add that I've created a number of information products, that I am a world traveler, a foodie, and any number of my passions. I said what I did in my headline because that is my target audience for my business.

Here's something, however, that you could consider for yourself. You could say something like, "I help IT professionals in Columbus, Ohio, generate more business, sales and success" – or something like that. In this example, you are telling people who you are, who you help, and how you

21

help them. This simple format is:

I help *X individuals* in *X region/industry/etc. do* XYZ.

Another example, "I help business professionals ongoing coaching and education in the Midwest." Or "throughout United States".

The more specific you can make your compelling headline, the better targeted the leads you will receive. The more specific the area or niche you target, you will actually get *more* business than if you make a broader more general headline trying to cover every industry in every corner of the world. Really try to narrow it down so your headline is very precise on who you are, who you help, and how you help them.

If you have multiple products, write your headline to cover the most popular, niche targeted areas.

Next, as seen below, you want to put in your ZIP Code because this is where your business is located.

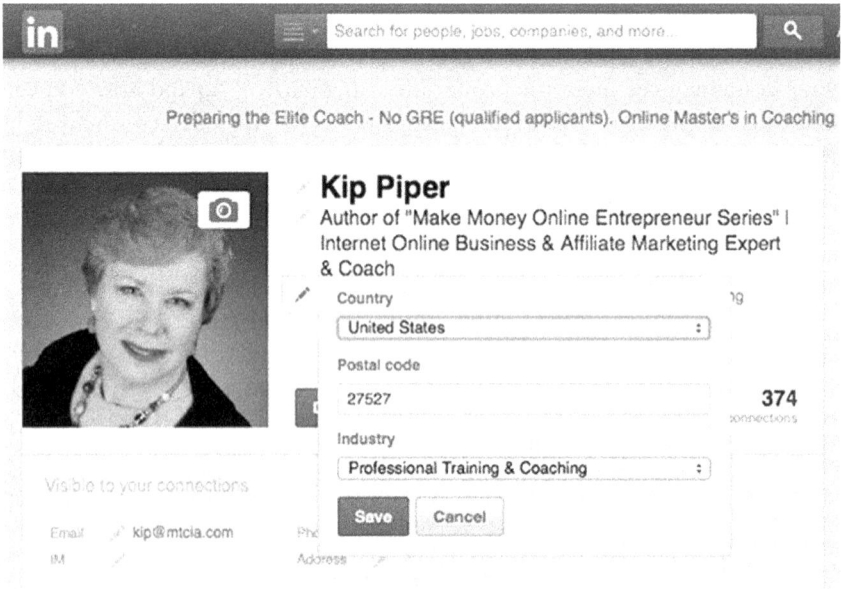

Finally, if you want to select your industry. There are a number of different industries from which to choose – however, you can choose only one. This will help you get even more leads by accurately selecting the industry you are in.

As a recap, in your headline you want to tell people who you are, who you help, and how you help them – in the least number of words. As you can see in my headline, I capitalized the primary words in the headline. This makes it look more like a headline and captures people's attention – much better than just a regular sentence.

WORK EXPERIENCE & RECOMMENDATIONS

In this chapter, we are going to cover your work experience and your recommendations.

Your work experience is a very important part of helping you not only get more business, when people research companies and adding you as connections, but also ranking you higher for certain keywords.

When people go to LinkedIn, they typically do one of two things:

- Search for people to hire
- Search for people to bring on as consultants

To accomplish this, they type in keywords in the "Search" field.

As an example, you could type in "affiliate marketing coach" in the search field. This is a very popular keyword and a large industry. My profile comes up on the first page – as the first result – out of almost 12,000 results. This means out of almost 12,000 people who have this keyword in their profile.

Obviously, this is a powerful keyword to rank for because a lot of people come to LinkedIn to do research to find experts in the affiliate marketing industry. When they conduct their search, they will find my profile, they will see my headline, and they will click on my profile to learn more about me. They will find out how I am connected to people, what groups I'm in, my past experience, where I work now. It is very powerful if you can rank high for your keywords, then a lot of people will start connecting with you and you will get more business and opportunities.

It is all about ranking first on LinkedIn for certain keywords. I will cover this some more later about how to rank higher for your keywords. You want to make sure you have in five main places, and I will go over those specific places later.

So let's get back to how to formulate your work experience. You want to list *all* of your current work experiences. Whether you have one job or five jobs, you want to add all of them because they are going to help you rank higher and will show people what you're up to. If you have just one position, that is fine! You may be working full-time for a company or have your own company. But if you are involved in a number of different things, such as having a side consulting business or other side business, be sure to add that in as well.

As you can see from my profile, I have a number of positions because I currently am involved in a variety of things – both business and personal. I also have a number of past work experiences which also help with keyword ranking on LinkedIn.

So here is what you want to do for your current work experience. You want to put your title in the form of a description, making sure to use your keywords. As you can see on my profile, I used the title "Internet Business Expert + Author + Trainer + Coach". You can also add the company name. Remember, your actual title is not as important as the keywords. If your keyword is "marketing professional", "business coach", "IT professional", "social media consultant", or whatever, you want to have that keyword in your current work experience. And you want to put that keyword in all your different current work experiences, as they apply. Make

27

sure that you use your keywords in your past work experience, also as they apply. Four instance, instead of my using a broad keyword such as "web designer" or "Internet marketer", I say that I am an "affiliate marketing coach" because that is the powerful keyword on which people search and are my target audience.

Remember, the "Title" is really the main description.

Company Name *

Title *

Location

Time Period *

Choose...   :   Year   —   Choose...   :   Year

☐ I currently work here

Description

See examples

Save   Cancel

The Title is where you're going to have the keywords for the description of your title. (In the "Description" section, you can include keywords, but it really doesn't help you rank higher by having those keywords in the description.) Your keywords must be in your current and past work experience Title in order to help you rank higher.

I frequently get asked how can someone make sure a certain position shows up as the first current work experience. There is no way to actually move or change the order of how your current work experience appears – if you have more than one current work experience listed. What you need to do is actually change the date of the one you want to appear first so it is the longest time you have been working there. So while you may not have been working the longest at the position you want to appear first, you need to go ahead and change the date so that it is at least one month longer then your next current experience.

The formatting of your Title – as a keyword rich description – applies both to your current and past work experience. So go ahead right now and update your current and work experience Titles for your chosen keywords.

It's important to add all of the past companies you work for because you never know who may be researching your profile. They may know the company, they may know people who worked at the company, and it may help you connect with them on a different level than someone who did not work at that company. This makes a smaller barrier of entry when they have some sort of reference or mutual connection – whether it is a company they recognize or someone they know who works there – they are more likely to connect with you than if they don't recognize the company you work for.

So make sure you include everything you can about your past work experience, and the keyword rich title and description, and also add as much of your current work experience which will help you rank higher on LinkedIn.

Now let's briefly go over recommendations.

Recommendations give you a lot of social proof. They help a lot, actually. Recommendations by people you're connected to and have written about you carries even more weight when a person who is your profile is connected to someone who's written you a recommendation – that's social proof! That shows that this person is credible, this person does good business, this person has a good product, is a good employee, etc.

The more recommendations you have, the better! While it does take a little time, it is very easy to build recommendations.

The number one way to build recommendations and to receive recommendations is to actually give first. That is actually the premise of LinkedIn – make sure you give as much as possible when you do anything on LinkedIn. (Actually, this applies to any social networking site and is good business practice in general.)

The goal is to give first, ask later.

To get recommendations, first reach out to people who you know who do good business, friends of yours, people you know will help you, authors and experts in your industry, etc. – and start recommending them!

You will find that about 50 to 60% of those for whom you write recommendations will write a recommendation back for you, without you ever having to ask for one. This is a very powerful method!

Not only do you begin to receive recommendations, but your name shows up on their profiles. You will then get connections from people because they will see your name on high powerful profiles for recommendations.

When you give a recommendation, LinkedIn automatically asks the other person when they receive the recommendation if they will be willing to give you one in return. So if you give a great recommendation, and 50 to 60% will feel inclined to give you one in return, they have done business with you and know you.

Obviously don't give a recommendation for someone you don't really know or hasn't helped you. In writing your recommendation, you want to be authentic and transparent – write from the heart.

The more recommendations you give, the more you will receive over time.

To give a recommendation, click on someone's profile and somewhere on the homepage. (As of this writing, you would to scroll down towards the bottom of their profile homepage to see some recommendations from others and a link to add your recommendation.) LinkedIn, as other social networking sites, is constantly changing, so you may have to search for it, but LinkedIn tries to make it obvious and easy to give a recommendation.

Your "Edit Profile" screen, you can manage your recommendations, as you can see below. You can rearrange their order or even delete any that you would like to not appear.

When you click on the "Manage Visibility" link to the right, a new screen opens, as you can see below, where you can perform a variety of tasks, such as view and manage your received and given recommendations. You can also ask to be recommended for specific positions. At the bottom, you can make a recommendation by searching by a person's name.

Take time to explore this section. You have the ability to request a new or updated recommendation from someone, you can manage and update recommendations that you have given, and you can ask to be recommended for specific things from people in your connections. (As I have said before, LinkedIn's interface is constantly changing. So I'm not going to include specific screenshots and instructions since they will most likely have changed by the time you read this.)

As you know, I prefer to give recommendations and receive unsolicited recommendations in return than ask for recommendations. However if you wish to ask for recommendation this is how you do it.

When you ask for a recommendation, you can send it out to up to 200 of your connections at one time. LinkedIn has done a great job to allow you to request recommendations from a very targeted group, so you're not wasting neither your own nor their time. You will also have a better chance of receiving great recommendations when you properly target the kind of recommendation, the industry, and the people within that industry.

Make sure you're asking recommendations from people that you know and they know you and/or have worked with you. To take the time to include a personal message to the person from whom you're asking the recommendation. Include in your personal note how you know them and why you feel their recommendation would be of value.

I reiterate that I preferred to give recommendations first instead of asking. I believe you will find that the quality of recommendations that you receive when you've given first will be much greater than those you have solicited.

So find 10 people you know on LinkedIn and give them great recommendations. You will be happy with the results!

YOUR WEBSITES

In this chapter, we will cover your websites as part of your LinkedIn profile.

When people come to your profile, they want to know what are your websites. LinkedIn offers you the option to designate a variety of different websites, such as, your blog, your company, personal, portfolio, other, etc., as you can see below.

However, the naming of your websites is a excellent opportunity to create calls to action and compelling headlines. To do this, choose "Other:" type of website from the drop-down menu. There you can add a custom title. Take this opportunity to add a call to action or compelling headline for your website.

As you can see from my profile, I added the custom titles "Affiliate Marketing Tips" and "Internet Online Business Tips". Now you know when you click on these links, you will be taken directly to the sections of my website which focus on these topics.

You want to have up to three websites – never just one website. If nothing else, then link to targeted sections with in your website to focus on niche topics, as I did with my tips links.

When you create your call to action or compelling headline for your website link, make sure you are using your chosen keywords. Here are a few examples:

- Download This Marketing Guide
- Free Tips On Webinar Marketing

34

- Free Email Course To Lose Weight

Then in the next field you will type in the actual URL of the website where you want to direct them to.

In my profile, instead of directing them just to my homepage, I provide the direct link to the affiliate marketing tips section of my website.

You can direct them to a blog page, or to a landing page, to a newsletter sign-up page, to an about page, to a resources page, to a contact page, etc.

If you send them to a contact page, then make your website headline a call to action, such as, "Call today for a free quote", or something similar and relevant. The more people that actually reach out and contact you from this link, ask for your service or product, the more sales you are going to make.

So use the headline for your website to tell people exactly where they need to go. You will get more inbound marketing from people connecting with you on LinkedIn!

YOUR SUMMARY & SPECIALTIES

In this chapter we will go over your summary and specialties.

The summary is the "meat" of your profile where you made your main compelling points of what you're trying to convey.

Just like the title of your profile, the summary needs to say who you are, who you help, and how you help them. You also want to include some type of call to action – such as, "Go To My Website", "Call My Office Number Here", "Download This Free Report" – you want to have a called action. You want to drive people to your website or another appropriate place where they can contact you, buy your products, go through a free coaching call, or whatever it may be, you want to drive them somewhere so you can get a result.

There are two different primary ways to create a summary. Remember, you can edit your summary and change things around at any time.

The first way to focus on the primary areas or projects for your business. As you can see from my profile, I have several different business and personal areas of interest and have separated them out into individual sections within the summary. I have used my chosen keywords in my section headlines. I also include a call to action to learn more about my publications and the coaching services I offer.

If you are a business where you take a lot of phone calls, put your phone number in your summary and tell people to call you. Be sure to include your specific hours exactly when people can contact you.

If you want them to email you, put your email address in here.

If you have just one the main focus, business, job or career, give people an insight to who you are. Tell what you are passionate about, what your goals are, what you like to do for fun, things like that to get people interested in you. People like stories, they like to learn more about you – not just reading a resume. In fact, the summary is *not* a resume – it is more of a professional/personal profile at the same time.

You have finished your short introductory paragraph, then add your first headline "This Is Who I Help:". And then write a short paragraph or two about who you specifically help – by industry, profession, geographic region, etc. For example, "I help small business owners in the IT industry in central Kansas." Be as specific as possible describing who you help.

Next headline is "This Is How I Help X:". In place of the "X", use the same specific job title or industry here, as you listed in the previous section. Four instance, "This Is How I Help Small Businesses".

Then you write one or two paragraphs describing specifically how you help them. For instance, "I help small business owners achieve their goals." "I create a specific step-by-step plan that helps them go from A to B." tell your reader exactly what they're going to get when they work with you.

Your next headline should be "This Is How To Learn More:". Specific instructions on how to visit your website, contact you, or both. You can also give them a call to action, such as, "Download This Free Guide", or "Sign Up For This Free Webinar", or something similar.

So think about which structure will work best for you and set up your summary right now. No matter which structure you choose, this format will make your profile look cleaner, helps you stand out from the crowd, and it will give you more leads and more sales setting up your summary this way.

Before I close this chapter, I want to make a few comments about the Specialties section of your summary. Specialties are an important part of your summary and the perfect place to use your keywords. You want to add keyword phrases throughout your Specialties section.

For instance, in my profile I list the specialties:

- Affiliate Marketing Expert & Coach
- Website & Blogging Coach
- Online Business Coach

I also list a couple of specialties that are part of my personal interests, but include them at the and of the list and keep my niche specialties at the top of the list.

CONNECTING WITH EVERYONE

In this chapter, we're going to go over your connections. To get to your connections, go to the top menu and hover over "Network", then select "Contacts", as you can see below.

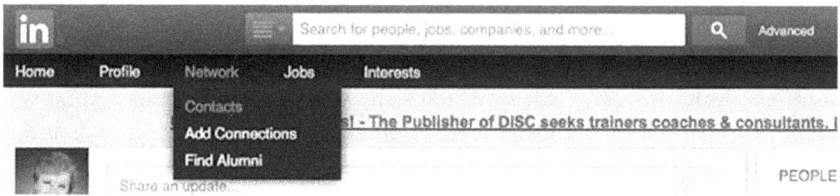

When you hover over "Network", you also see "Add Connections". We will go over "Add Connections" later.

In my opinion, it's important to connect with everyone on LinkedIn. Every day I get invites from people on LinkedIn. I connect with all of them for basically one reason – you can export all of your connections. To do so, click on the settings wheel in the upper right corner of your LinkedIn page, as seen below.

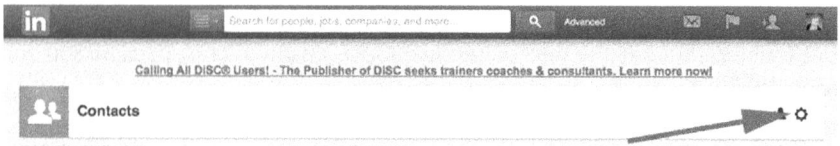

Then click on the "Export LinkedIn Connections" link on the right-hand side, as seen below.

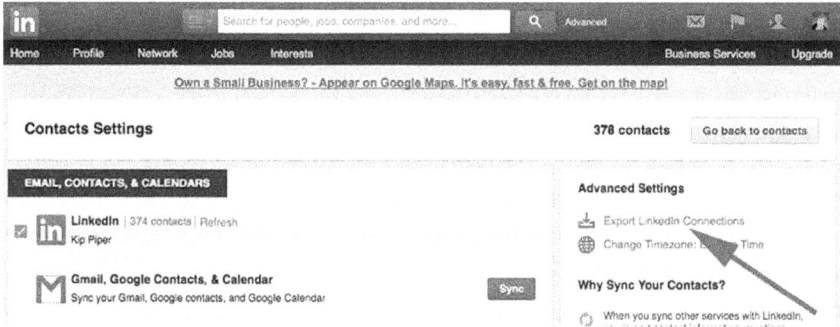

Oh then see the screen below, where you can select to export all of your connections in a variety of formats.

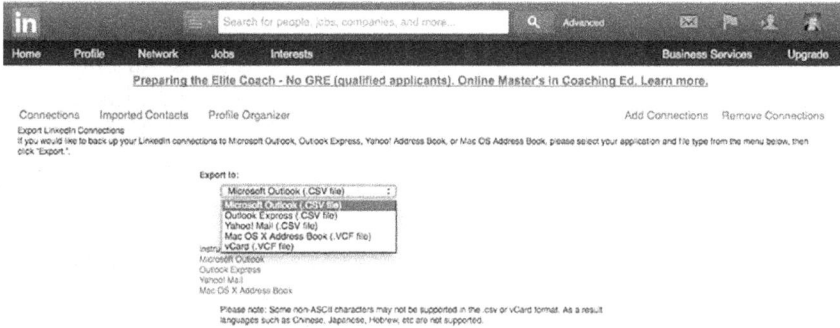

The most universal format is a CSV file, which you can save to your computer. You can then import the CSV file into other email programs or into your email management service.

This means you can import all of your LinkedIn connections into your email marketing campaign and send messages to those your connected to on LinkedIn.

A great way to organize your connections beyond the basic categories that LinkedIn offers (company, location, title, source) to create Tags for the different ways you want to categorize your contacts.

You can tag a person when they become a new connection, or you can edit a current connection by either adding them to a current tag category or creating a new tag category or editing a current category, as seen below.

Sort by Last Name ▾   aZ ▾   Filter by All Contacts ▾   Q Search

Select All

Sonja (Smith) Das 1st
Sr. Team Leader at Essential Bodywear Rep
Austin, Texas Area
🏷 friends
🏷 Tag ✉ Message More ▾

classmates
colleagues   77 1st
✓ friends   Feng Shui Research Center, USA
group_members
partners
+ Add New Tags   inting Software, Inc.
⟳ Manage Tags
🏷 friends

I recommend you keep the number of connections within each category limited to 50. This is because you can message within LinkedIn only up to 50 people at a time. This makes it an easy way to send a LinkedIn message to 50 people at a time.

Where this comes in handy is if you want to create an event around a certain group of people, say, within a certain targeted location in the country, like just people in your city. So you create a tag category for people who are within the geographic area you want to target. You can then add the appropriate connections to this tag category.

You can also categorized by industry, and then send targeted messages to the connections within that industry tag category.

There are two schools of thought about adding connections. Some people only want to add those they know, like and trust – friends, family, and those with whom they have done business. I can appreciate this train of thought.

For me, and possibly for you as an online business owner or entrepreneur, I want to build a network as large as possible. But my goals maybe different than yours.

You need to figure out what are your goals and how do you want to build, manage and communicate with your LinkedIn network.

Basically, the more people you're connected to, the more people in the second and third degree network who can find you. (The second and third degree network are the people who are connected to the people you're connected to.)

When the people in the second and third degree networks are searching LinkedIn, they are more likely to find you, contact you, and then hire you or purchase your services or products.

Next let's cover adding connections. From the top menu, you hover over "Network" and then click on "Add Connections", as you can see below.

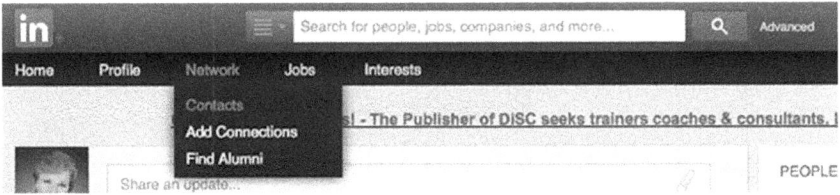

LinkedIn may ask you to enter your password again. On the next screen, you can add contacts from your Gmail, your Outlook, your Yahoo email, etc., as you can see below.

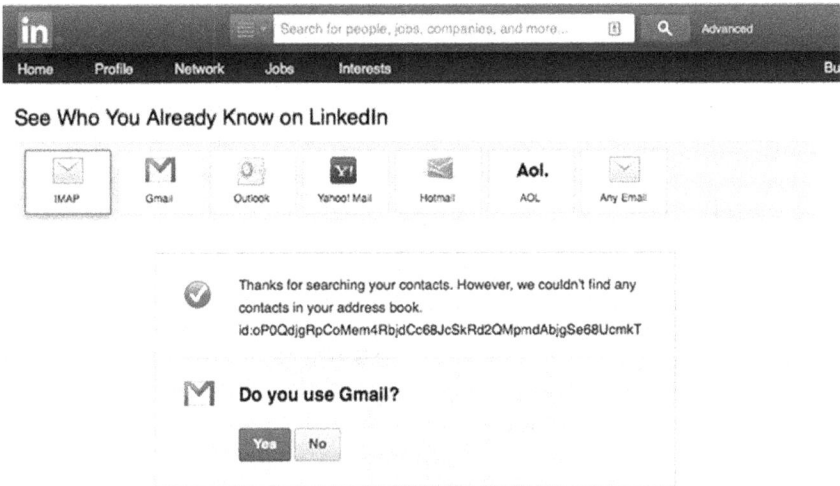

Depending on how many people you have in these different accounts, it may take a little time.

NOTE: You do *not* have to use this tool if you do not wish to! I have chosen not to because I have already selected the contacts on my various email accounts and have connected with them on LinkedIn. As I make new contacts in my business and other areas of my life, I manually connect with them via LinkedIn.

When reviewing the list captured by LinkedIn, make sure you are connecting *only* with those that already are on LinkedIn and with whom you have *not* yet connected with via LinkedIn.

When you have finished making your selections, LinkedIn will then send the email to those contacts inviting them to connect with you on LinkedIn.

THE POWER OF GROUPS: JOINING

In this chapter, we're going to discuss finding and joining groups. Groups are a huge part of LinkedIn and they are a big part of my business and other people's businesses.

Specifically, we're going to discuss finding different groups in your niche – finding the right groups to join.

You're going to start by clicking on the drop down to the left of the search field at the top of your LinkedIn screen, as seen below, and click on "Groups".

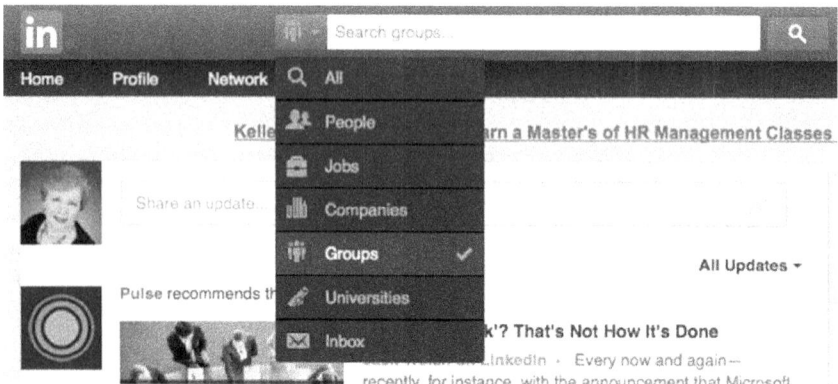

Then in the search field, type in the keyword for your niche or industry. For me, I would type in "affiliate marketing" or "online business". As you can see from the image below, there are almost 600 affiliate marketing LinkedIn groups.

Now I can narrow this down to a smaller number of groups by entering a more targeted keyword. So I changed the keyword to "affiliate marketing training" and ended up with only 13 groups, as seen below.

It's okay to end up with a large number of groups in your search results. You *want* to the join lots of appropriate related groups in your niche.

Once you have your niche groups search results, you want to join the bigger groups first. These are the ones where you can tap into a network because these larger groups already have established networks of thousands of people. Would you rather join a group of several thousand people or only 25 people? You are more likely to get more out of the group with several thousand members.

You can also search groups by geographic location, such as your city, state, or geographic region.

After you become a member of a group, there are lots of things you can do – which I will cover in detail in the next chapter about creating your own groups. You can do things like add a discussion, start a discussion, attach a link, post your articles – things that will help you drive more traffic to your website, to your opt-in page, to your events page, etc. You can write comments, you can like different things, you can really engage the audience in that niche-related group. There are lots of different ways to get your name out there. You are getting exposure to the members of this group and it's very targeted exposure. The more people who comment on your post, then the higher post is ranked. So you want to keep people active in the discussion created by your post.

I encourage you to go through and see who are the members of the group. Where do they work? What do they do? How many people do they have in their network? You can even do an advanced search to see which people in your group you are already connected to and those with whom you're not yet connected. You can also do an advanced search to see who works at a specific company, where they are located, and a ton of other ways to conduct an advanced search. This is a very powerful way to target exactly who you want to find and who the people are within your groups.

THE POWER OF GROUPS: CREATING GROUPS

In this chapter, we're going to talk about the next big thing to make your LinkedIn experience powerful for your business – creating your own groups.

Why is creating a group powerful? Why is it important to have your own group?

When you create your own group, you draw to you other LinkedIn professionals who are interested in or involved in the niche targeted by your group. As the group creator, you have full control over the group, what is said, and even editing powers to delete inappropriate discussions.

You can even create subgroups to the main group, such, as niche markets that target areas of interest of the main group.

For instance, you could have an online business group and then have subgroups in the niche markets of affiliate marketing, product creation, email marketing, etc. You could even have subgroups targeting specific product areas, such as, affiliate marketing training programs, email marketing service providers, etc.

You can communicate with all of the members within your group. So once a week, or whatever schedule you prefer, you could send a custom broadcast message to everyone within your group. This gives you the opportunity to regularly network with everyone within your group – where they see your name, your website, and a personal message from you. Very powerful!

Other things you can do as the group creator are:

- You can customize the group interface with a logo
- You can send invitations to other LinkedIn professionals to join your group
- You can preapprove people as group members – specifically set your group settings to open access which automatically accepts

new members
- You can add group managers
- You can manage templates
- You can send direct messages to individual members of the group
- You can scroll through, review and search the members of the group
- You can see how you're connected to each member of the group
- You can remove members from the group
- And tons of other custom settings

To create a group, hover over in the "Interests" link in the top menu and then click on "Groups", as you can see below.

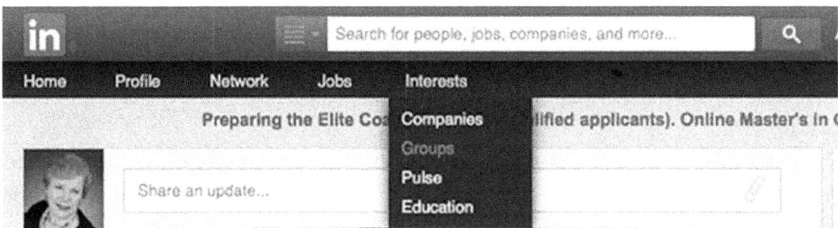

Once on the Groups page, simply click on the link at left to "Create a group", as shown below.

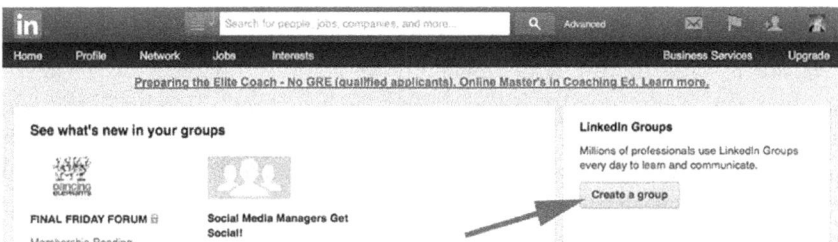

As creator of the group, you can call the group anything you want. However, considering that the group name will be picked up by and ranked on Google, you want to use your best keyword in the name of the group. Using your best keyword, the link to your group will rank higher on Google.

In choosing the group type, it is best to choose either "networking" or "professional". You can choose other categories if you wish, but I have found it best for growing your business and your LinkedIn presence to use either "networking" or "professional".

When writing your Summary, keep it to just a couple of paragraphs. Make it very clear very clear for whom this group is designed and the benefits they will receive by being the members of the group. Then in your Description, include a call to action, such as visiting a website, a link to download a free report, a link to watch a video, etc.

Under the Website field, make sure you put in your actual website, if you have one (and you should!). This is not required but is a great marketing strategy.

Under Access, select "Auto-join". This is a great timesaver in that it keeps you from having to manually approve each person who requests to join the group. In addition, when they join, they receive an instant message from you (from your welcome message template, which is discussed below) and gives them instant access to the group, which is a great first impression for building a relationship.

Since you want to build the biggest network possible, do not choose "Location". When you choose Location, LinkedIn limits your group to a location-based parameter. It is best to leave the group open to the whole world. You can always later create subgroups for specific geographic areas, if you wish.

Let's take a moment and talk about templates. Templates are automated messages that you create for a variety of functions, such as, the welcome message when someone joins your group. You can customize these templates with your own subject line and message. This is an important step for members who join your group in making them feel welcome and building your relationship with them.

In your welcome message template, you can also start your marketing relationship with the group member. You can encourage them to go to your website to sign up for your email list or your opt-in page or whatever landing page is appropriate. You ask them to like you on Facebook and add you on Twitter. With this strategy, you are getting the people who join your group to opt-in outside of LinkedIn to your email list and other social networking sites. This gives you the opportunity to engage with your customers, your audience, and your niche in a more targeted fashion. You can keep them up-to-date on what you're doing all the time.

If you wish, you can create multiple groups. As of this writing, however, LinkedIn limits to 10 the number of groups you can create. So choose wisely!

You can also add your RSS feed from your blog to your LinkedIn group. This will automatically post any new articles on your blog to the discussions feed in your LinkedIn group. This helps stimulate conversation and activity in your group (as well as the convenience of not having to copy and paste your article information into your LinkedIn group).

Next, let's discuss growing your group. I am regularly asked the big question, "How you get members into your group?" It's easy to create a group – anyone can do that. But how do you grow your group and really build it to a large number of members?

When you first start your group, it goes back to the basics of building direct connections with people. Once you're connected with someone, send them an invitation from within the group owner interface inviting them to join the group (LinkedIn automatically includes a link to your group) – *if* your group is appropriate for that person's areas of interest, business, or niche.

When you write your invitation to join the group, be sure to include reasons why they should enjoy the group, such as, who the group is for and the benefits of being in the group. You want to entice them to join the group.

If you are already connected with a lot of people on LinkedIn, then be sure to sort your connections by industry or tag category so you are targeting appropriate niches with your group invitation.

You can grow your group by promoting it in the other LinkedIn groups in which you are a member. Another way to grow your group is to be sure to include a link to join your LinkedIn group on all of your appropriate websites. Also include this link on all of your email broadcasts and newsletters, your business card, your business email signature, your Facebook page/profile/groups/lists, and your Twitter account, etc. If you are a member of niche-related forums on the Internet (and you should be!), you can send invitations to your fellow forum members.

The best way is to first, foremost and always invite your LinkedIn connections to your group.

ADVANCED STRATEGIES

This chapter is all about the advanced strategies to close deals, make connections, and better build your LinkedIn relationships – both online and off-line. We will discuss sending invitations, researching profiles and finding the right people, making introductions, and taking it "offline" so you can turn it into a business transaction.

As an example, let's say were looking for someone in the marketing department at a major real estate company. So I type in "real estate" in the People section of the search box, as shown below.

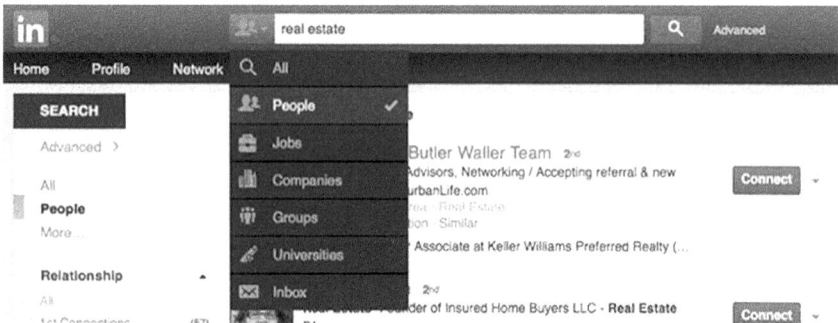

You can also search for Jobs, Companies, Groups, etc. For this example, let's do People to start, since we are looking for individuals working for a major real estate company. As you can see below, there are over 4 million search results for people who have "real estate" in their profile.

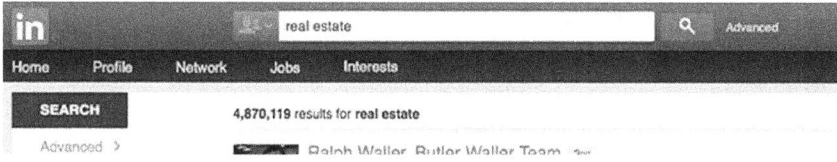

This could be for a number of reasons. People could say their interest is real estate, they used to work in real estate, etc. So you may not find everyone you want to connect with on the first search results. Let's try to narrow it down a little bit.

By selecting certain parameters in the left column, as shown below, I narrowed the search by choosing, 1st and 2nd degree connections and Keller Williams Realty.

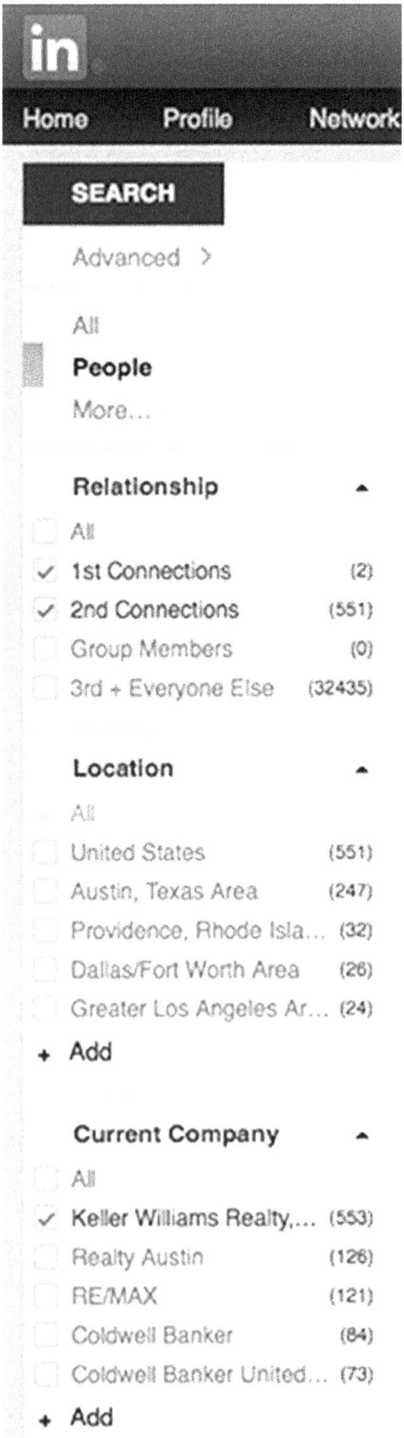
in
Home
Profile
Network
SEARCH
Advanced >
All
People
More…
Relationship
All
1st Connections (2)
2nd Connections (551)
Group Members (0)
3rd + Everyone Else (32435)
Location
All
United States (551)
Austin, Texas Area (247)
Providence, Rhode Isla… (32)
Dallas/Fort Worth Area (26)
Greater Los Angeles Ar… (24)
+ Add
Current Company
All
Keller Williams Realty,… (553)
Realty Austin (126)
RE/MAX (121)
Coldwell Banker (84)
Coldwell Banker United… (73)
+ Add

When I selected 1st and 2ⁿᵈ degree connections, it reduced the number of results down to 26,010. When I then selected Keller Williams Realty, it reduced my results down to 553.

As you can see from the image above, you can narrow your search results even further by selecting more or different parameters, like levels of connections, by location, by company, industry, etc.

When I never the search by industry and marketing and advertising, it reduced my search results to 208.

Near the top of my results was a LinkedIn member with whom I am not connected but we have three shared connections. When I clicked on the "3 shared connections" link, it opened up the window to show the specific connections, as you can see below.

You can research this way to find out who are your shared connections and expand your connections by requesting to connect with them. Plus, I now have a person I can contact in real estate marketing and advertising, and introduce myself to her as having mutual connections on LinkedIn. Before contacting her, I would conduct more research about her, such as, check out her interests, what school she attended, etc., to establish mutual points of reference or conversation openers. I would try to find two or three things in common that we have and with which I can connect with her to drop the entry barrier and immediately start a relationship.

This is a person you probably don't know. They may get dozens of emails from people asking similar things. You have to break through that noise. So the psychology is to break down any barrier first by finding a way to connect to that person on a deeper, intimate level – whether it's through their friends, through different associations, through hobbies, etc.

The key in sending this text message is to connect with the person first – you're not trying to pitch them anything – then try to learn more about them by letting them know you are wanting to connect with them and talk with them about what did they do and how you may be able to help them.

With this approach, especially with the offer to help them – not pitch to them – you are increasing your chances for a positive response, for that person remembering your name. So you connect with them first, get to know them better, and *only* talk about different business topics or ideas further down the line.

The mutual connections is most powerful. When you can connect names to people and experiences, you're going to be able to get an email or phone call in response and ultimately close deals.

SUMMARY

In this book we've gone through the different aspects of Linkedin:

- How to set up your profile
- How to make connections
- How to join groups
- How to create your own group
- Advanced strategies

Linkedin is a great resource to find business owners and entrepreneurs who identify themselves in particular niches.

Remember, you need to understand whether your business is business-to-business or business-to-consumer.

If you are business-to-consumer, you want to leverage LinkedIn to build your presence, find potential affiliates, and generally network to gain exposure.

If you are business-to-business – whether a single entrepreneur or a multinational company – you will be able to potentially sell directly on LinkedIn.

It's important to understand how your business specifically fits in LinkedIn.

One of the things I always recommend with all social media networking accounts and profiles – whether it's Twitter, Facebook, LinkedIn, and even YouTube – you want to convert the traffic, your fan base, your connections, your followers onto your email list. Then you can market to them more directly, put them into your sales funnel, promote your sales pages or affiliate offers, etc.

The biggest thing with LinkedIn, as with any social media networking site, create a general strategy using the information in this book. Also, social media is easy to outsource, so find a virtual assistant or an employee in your office who can manage your connections, send out your invitations, and other routine tasks.

BONUS MATERIALS

Below are links to this book's bonus materials. I have developed these tools from my own experience as well as compiled from tools I have used from various training courses I have taken.

The mind map is built in XMind software. You can download a free version of XMind from **http://www.xmind.net**.

The item is also available as a PDF.

Strategic_Plan_List_Building_with_LinkedIn.xmind
http://www.kippiperbooks.com/make-money-online/book10/Strategic_Plan_List_Building_with_LinkedIn.xmind

Strategic_Plan_List_Building_with_LinkedIn.pdf
http://www.kippiperbooks.com/make-money-online/book10/Strategic_Plan_List_Building_with_LinkedIn.pdf

RESOURCES

Make Money Online Entrepreneurs LinkedIn Group

I invite you to join my group! Simply visit this URL:
http://www.linkedin.com/groups/Make-Money-Online-Entrepreneurs

LinkedInfluence by Lewis Howes

This **advanced** LinkedIn course teaches you how to effectively optimize your profile, manage your groups, and how to make LinkedIn really work for you for your business and optimize it for the most marketing value. Here is the URL to learn more:

http://kippiperbooks.com/LinkedInfluence

Book 1 – Freeing Up Your Time – VA's, Outsourcing & Goal Setting
http://www.kippiperbooks.com/book1

MORE KINDLE BOOKS BY KIP PIPER

Ultimate Affiliate Marketing with Blogging Quick Start Guide
http://www.kippiperbooks.com/UltimateGuide

Make Money Online Entrepreneur Series:

Below are just a few of the books in this series. To browse the entire series, go to:

http://www.kippiperbooks.com/makemoneyonlineseries

Book 1 – Freeing Up Your Time – VA's, Outsourcing & Goal Setting
http://www.kippiperbooks.com/book1
Book 2 – Your Core Business, Niche & Competitors
http://www.kippiperbooks.com/book2
Book 3 – Blogs & Emails: Your Link with Your Customers
http://www.kippiperbooks.com/book3
Book 4 – Affiliate Marketing 101
http://www.kippiperbooks.com/book4
Book 5 - Driving Traffic with Organic SEO
http://www.kippiperbooks.com/book5
Book 6 – Power of Email Marketing
http://www.kippiperbooks.com/book6
Book 7 – Quick Income Formula with Advanced Affiliate Marketing
http://www.kippiperbooks.com/book7
Book 8 – List Building with Facebook
http://www.kippiperbooks.com/book8
Book 9 – List Building with Twitter
http://www.kippiperbooks.com/book9

ONE LAST THING…

As you can probably tell from my writing, my intention is to inspire and support more people to build a better financial future. It's a tough economy today, and I think personal growth in the field of small business is more important than ever before. Even though I have well over 20 years of experience as a successful small business owner and online entrepreneur, I don't have all the answers. In fact I'm still learning myself, I just have my own opinions, experiences and a passion for being my own boss to guide me through life.

Thank you purchasing my eBook and for taking the time to read it. I hope you enjoyed it and found value within its pages.

If you did I would really appreciate your support by taking the time to write a review for me on Amazon. Reviews really help the authors you enjoy to get noticed in a crowded marketplace, and it would allow me to continue writing the books for this series and other business books.

Please visit the URL below to let me know your thoughts:

www.kippiperbooks.com/book10

All of my books are offered completely FREE on the launch and I want to reward loyal readers by offering my new books to them FREE of charge when they are released.

So please visit my website **www.KipPiperBooks.com** and either download your free copy of *"28-Day Small Business Profit Plan: The Quick Start Guide to Business Success"* or just sign up to my newsletter in order to be kept informed when the next release is due. I hate spam, so I promise I won't share your information with anyone – not for love nor money!

Good luck! I wish you every success in your personal and business endeavors.

www.ingramcontent.com/pod-product-compliance
Lightning Source LLC
Chambersburg PA
CBHW070826210326
41520CB00011B/2140